中国当代艺术家画传
李梦 绘

LI MENG

李梦

PURE GENERATION

纯色一代

U0095048

目录

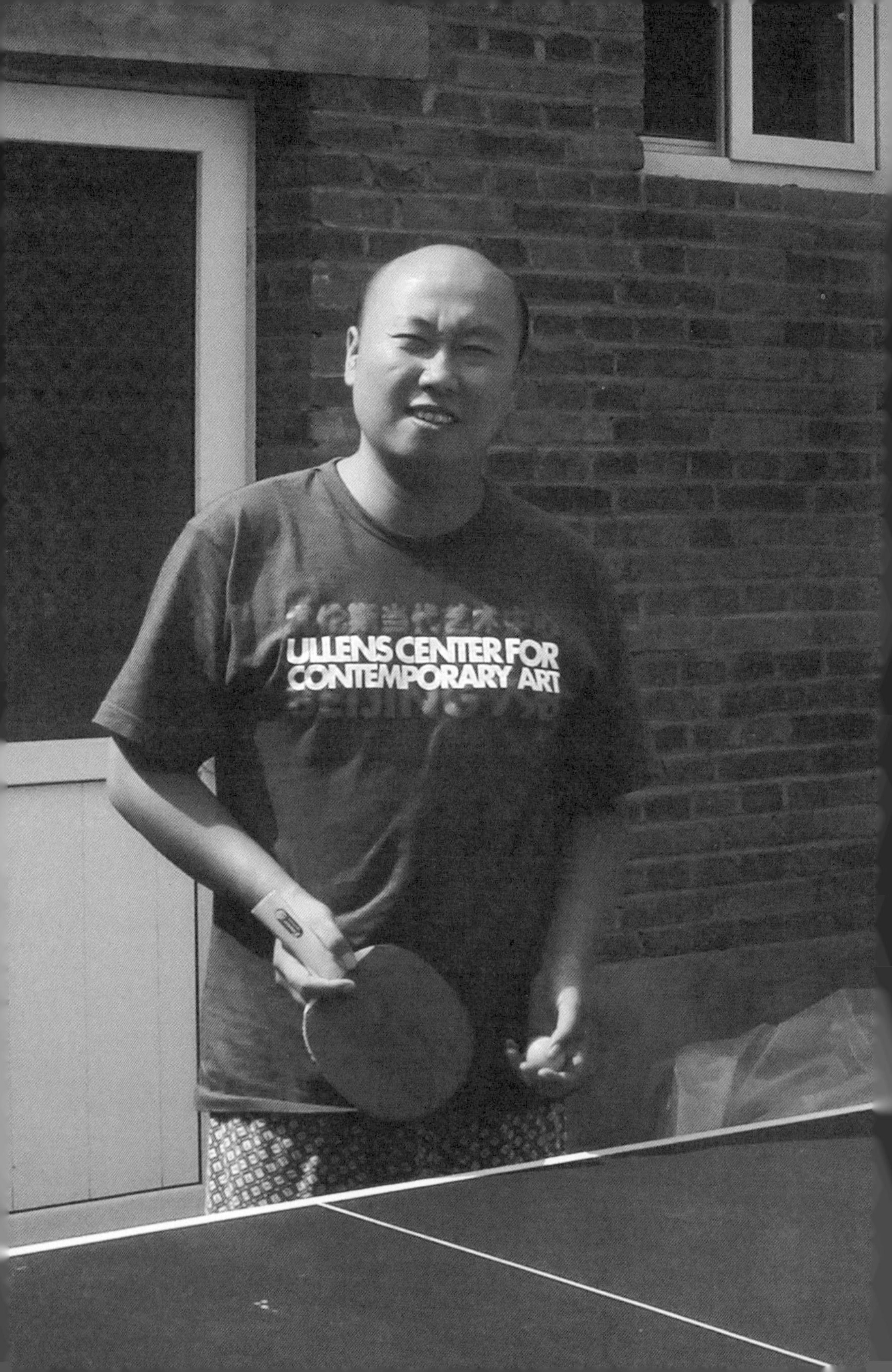
ULLENS CENTER FOR
CONTEMPORARY ART

李梦
北京人

1980年2月8日出生于辽宁营口市
1999年毕业于中央工艺美院附属中学
2003年毕业于天津科技大学环境艺术设计专业

作品参展

<u>2006年</u>
意大利博洛尼亚国际艺术博览会
法国佩里格市弗朗索瓦密特朗国家艺术中心

<u>2007年</u>
北京中艺博国际艺术博览会
上海艺术博览会
纽约Chelsea画廊区、Gagosian画廊举行联合展览
巴塞尔博览会威尼斯双年展
卡塞尔文献展
中国年轻艺术家当代油画展
Barry LeVa 纽约画廊
纽约Alp画廊
"La Cina è vicina"那波利美术馆

<u>2008年</u>
北京798艺术区参加联合画展

重要收藏
中国美术馆
今日美术馆
何香凝美术馆

纯色一代

我们是 80 后的一代人，这一代是让人喜爱、受人重视的一代人。由于残酷的对外部世界和自我内部的生存竞争，在从家庭、学校到社会的成长环境下，我们整个民族的现代代际特征几乎没有摆脱过各种层次的仇恨和苦难感，但在 80 后一代人身上这些代际特征好像一夜之间消失了。

随着"超级女声"、刘翔、姚明、韩寒等 80 后一代偶像的现身，80 后一代的艺术也正紧跟着登场了。考虑到可能引起的歧义，我自己更愿意用"纯色的一代"来命名 80 后的一代艺术人。自 19 世纪末中国进入现代世界后，中华民族几乎没有真正拥有过这种集体性的世代特征。这种所谓的"纯色"，是指他们身上正在出现我们这个民族几千年来都没有达到过的、一系列的、开放的、社会的自我特征：轻松、幽默、自信、敏锐、可爱、性开放和信息交通自由化所带来的国际化和自我真实感等。

这是 80 后一代值得我们喜爱和重视的重要原因之一，他们的艺术已经来了，并体现出了一种先兆！80 后的绘画、雕塑和 Video 艺术受西方前卫艺术的直接影响较少。最为可贵的是他们的艺术气质也如同整个 80 后一代的代际特征，即很少有那种苦大仇深、自我痛苦和凝重的视觉特征。他们重新塑造了新一代的自我特质：自我为中心、超级幻想、游戏人生、可爱等等，在视觉上具有一种纯真的、向上的、冲击的力量。

与 20 世纪 50 年代至 70 年代出生的人相比，80 后的这一代人也许没有什么特别的、深厚的文化基础。他们生活在电视、影碟、CD 音乐、酒吧、卡拉 OK、时尚街、电脑和互联网、电子游戏以及体育和旅游等等各方面条件充足的时代，对于大多数人而言，读书只能占据青春生命期的一小部分时间，他们更多地需要是去深入生活其中，细细地实践、体会和体验，这也就促成了 80 后的感觉特别敏锐和感情特别细腻。而 80 后的艺术，也因此在形式和自我特征上开始真正具有中国本土的当代特征。

进行代际比较的话，上几代人的艺术几乎在传统延续和西方文化拿来之间，进行苦苦挣扎的徘徊过程中，寻求本土化的出路，但这种本土化主要停留在符号和政治意识形态的观念层次，很难在经验层面上日常化和感觉化。而80后艺术则真正体现在日常视觉和自我感觉的层次上，他们似乎轻而易举地获得了上几代苦求不得的既中国又当代的图像特征，这种本土气质和形式特征无疑是一种真正意义上的当代原产的自我分泌物。

80后艺术表现了新世纪以来中国正在形成中的超级结构中的体系经验和自我特征，实际上在"超女"和姚明、刘翔的身上已经体现出80后一代的成长背景。湖南卫视的中国流行歌曲偶像节目"超级女声"表明了中国不仅在资本、劳动力流动和生产规模上有所超越，即使在流行文化的商业化和娱乐化程度上也在超越美国等资本主义国家。

与上一代相比，70后文学以及70后艺术还反映着这一代人在中国社会转型时期的特征，比如凝重、现实、残酷、自我中心。在贾樟柯的电影中，北方城市经历着从县城、小城向现代都市的变化，但这种都市还没有完全形成，还处在县城文化和都市布局的交错中。在棉棉的小说中，来自西方的现代知识分子和精英文化已经被同样来自西方的摇滚乐、酒吧和青春残酷的城市生活所取代，就像村上春树的小说人物一样，这一代不再关心真理以及对于世界和他人的拯救，而是开始关注自我感觉和纯粹青春的个人情感宿命，但是这一代仍然具有上一代的遗传痕迹，他们一毕业就置身于现实秩序的崩溃和社会财富巧取豪夺的最初的残酷进程中，比如无序社会的道德受伤、对于现实的残酷、都市冷漠的自我脆弱感，并由此具有一些对于社会现实的仇视。

80后一代的成长期正好是中国改革开放以后经济、文化、生活等各个方面快速的成长时期。社会已经完成了新的超级解构期，人们从过去社会结构中解脱出来，各种观念、意识在新的社会形态下逐渐转变，在这种溃散、转变的过程中伴随的新生的苦痛没有影响、延续到这一代。80后一代多为独生子女，享受着多方面、全方位的宠爱，也正因为此我们变得可亲、可爱，对他人和社会怀有善意，对事物抱着一颗爱心。80后一代因物质小康和社会安定免受上一代的身体劳作和变迁之苦，因此更多进入精神之轻和超验想象的解脱之路。这是我们民族人性进步的一个新起点，实际上也是80后艺术超越上一代的一个自我基础。

与杨少斌先生在一起

和高中同学杨旭在我的工作室

在ART18和朋友们在一起

我们享受了前所未有的开放、进步、物质、消费、媒体和关爱。我们可以坐飞机或驾车，去到另一个城市工作、旅游，有时是参加其他省市电台的选秀节目，而且也有可能意外出名，成为年轻的明星和百万富翁。

我们是充满梦想的一代，正好生在能够实现梦想的时代。

80后艺术实际上真正体现出这一代的成长和自我特征。即80后一代的成长期主要是在新世纪这6年，正好是中国基本上完成了结构性转型，最终形成并将在相当长一段时期保持双性社会的文化特征和体制结构。80后一代从一开始就享受了极高的物质生活和精神生活，我们包围充斥着各种各样的、眼花缭乱的新景象、新事物——手机、网络、邮箱、信用卡、提款机、酒吧、文化园区、798艺术工厂、宋庄艺术园区等等。由于大学的扩招、娱乐文化事业的发展、跨国公司的大规模进入、私人汽车的普及、社会传媒化以及明星崇拜等等，物质消费和城市设施地方差异的缩小，使得80后的艺术人可以放开视角与世界最前沿的艺术相通，与最有实力的画廊合作，最大可能的实现了我们的艺术梦想。

生于1981年的方亦秀和邓瑜都毕业于广州美术学院，他们画的是道路、小人、树、小动物、小家具、星星、月亮等，这些产自他们成长经验的像钥匙或手机挂件的小玩偶图案又被用各种线条和网状结构连接和布局，放在各种酷流行颜色的画布背景上，有趣的是邓瑜使用的颜料不是专业颜料，而是各种色彩的指甲油。他们的画只是一种具有卡通图像特征的绘画，但很难归入写实抽象或者涂鸦绘画的范畴。

很难说他们的绘画是为了表达某种意义，但也很难说他们的画不具有新的意义。画面的图案、色调和布局的把握主要是靠自我感觉、情趣和在广州这个卡通文化很早普及的城市的成长经验，他们实际上很少有确定的绘画技术和技巧，但这有时候似乎更难把握。这种绘画主要是一种心灵分泌的形式，它当然具有国际卡通文化的特征，但同时也很中国，与日本、美国的卡通绘画特征还是有区别。

申大鹏的绘画体现出80后一代的成长和自我肖像特征：学校上空依然飘扬着红旗，有夹着公文包从校园围栏外走过的老师，一男一女两个学生坐着，好像没有经历过什么生活磨难和社会变革，但经历了一场场考试，楞得可爱又自我中心的表情，穿着卡通 T 恤，表现出一种衣食无忧不在乎任何人的纯真感，却显得别有一种纯真力量。申大鹏生于 1982 年，毕业于天津美术学院，这是一个绘画专业水平长期排位较低的美院，但是他的超级写实能力却奇迹般出挑，不用说在八大美院，就是拿到欧美也不算差。

对语言的技术品质的迷恋和细腻品质，80 后一代好像一下子超出了上几代画家，这方面的另一个代表就是毕业于湖北美术学院的 WAZA 小组。这个小组一共 6 个人，基本上出生于 1982 年、1983 年。他们的 3D 动画短片获得 2006 年杭州国际动漫博览会一等奖。这个短片中虚拟了美国歌星迈克尔·杰克逊去武汉访问的一段电视访谈节目，还虚拟了一个小歌迷在电视上用武汉方言唱的一段关于武汉当代市井文化的无厘头表演。

WAZA 小组全靠自学掌握了 3D 动画技术，他们的艺术准则是这一代人一定要重视语言的技术品质，在电子媒体时代，技术本身就是一种语言。这一点他们几乎要比其他 80 后艺术家自觉得多。由于电子媒体和都市文化的地方差异的缩小，天津和武汉这些原先艺术语言落后和文化气质显得"土"气的地方，却具有很国际化的语言和图像特质，如申大鹏和 WAZA 小组的艺术作品，这也是 80 后艺术一个独特现象。

这一代成长于高度发达的物质环境、文化多元开放性和国际性最高的时代，他们更多享受了资本主义和社会主义这种双性社会的优点，使得 80 后一代一开始对处于复兴和上升时期的中国有一种发自内心的认同感，他们的作品很少有上几代人的艺术中出现的对于中国现实的讽刺和贬低。

生于 1981 年的高瑀毕业于四川美术学院，他重新塑造了 80 后特征的熊猫形象，体现了 80 后一代的精神隐喻：他们长在红旗下，但这面红旗不再是腥风血雨的飘扬在战场上千疮百孔的红旗，而是迎风飘扬的像广告旗一样红得发酷的红旗。他们迷恋那种虚拟的血淋淋的感觉，憧憬情人和爱情，显露出面对无间道现实的郁闷和无奈，具有仰慕中国传统的特性。高瑀的绘画有些冠以政治和传统的标题，但几乎都被低和浅的图像游戏风格所轻漫化，比如《抛头颅，洒鲜血》表现的是一只只流淌着鲜血做着鬼脸很漂

青春故事

亮的熊猫头；《隐士之死》是一只在清风漫舞的林阴下死得可爱安详的熊猫；《悠久的文化开出灿烂的花》则是一幅向传统致敬的漫画象征。传统的重负和政治的残酷，对于这一群长在红旗下的小熊猫们，则好像是一种只跟"符号"有关的精神现实。

郭文的绘画是向传统山水画的致敬。与前辈画家为改造绘画向现代转型而沉重的变革相比，他则显得轻松而有灵气。他将山水主题改成"山火"，让中国传统山水图像中的山顶燃起了一团火，在山脚下还出现了穿三点式和短裤游泳的时尚男女。

金钕的雕塑具有一种感伤唯美的视觉风格，她更倾向于青春魔幻的感伤主义风格。她的《长大——惘》是一个半人半马的雕塑，上半身是一个忧伤的美少女，在造型上有点类似日本电子游戏中的美少女形象，只是她的眼角流着泪，比始终快乐而斗志昂扬的电子游戏少女显得要脆弱和容易受伤得多。下半身是一条腿蹬地，另一条腿像一个贵族少女一样优雅地抬起在半空的马。金钕毕业于中央美术学院雕塑系，她的雕塑反映了这一代的自我精神是一种关于童话的记忆，而不是上一代人的关于革命和神话的启蒙。

尽管如此，80后一代似乎还是感觉有先天缺陷和不满足，比如不断地学习和考试，不再有社会动荡和革命性的变迁带来的深刻体验，而处在富足社会的生命之轻、贫富分化。高瑀的一幅画表现的是一只巨型熊猫像一个空虚青年在自虐，它用刀扎自己的眼睛，割下自己的生殖器。1981年出生的罗丹是著名画家罗中立的儿子。罗中立的油画表现了一个苦难深重的父亲形象，被批评界誉为代表了中国一代人的形象。而罗丹似乎决意表现这个父亲的孙子作为 80 后一代的形象，正拿着话筒宣泄式地唱摇滚乐，他并不表现为一个 20 世纪 60 年代式的波西米亚青年，他似乎只是渴望这一代人缺失的革命和激情。

新世纪以来的这个时期可以称作是"超级经验"的中国，80 后一代正成长在我们这个民族五千年以来从未经历的时期。尽管上几代成年人也在同时经历这个时代，但他们还具有历史的痛苦记忆和责任重负，而 80 后一代没有。我们一开始就成长于一个新的成型的经济和文化的超级结构，这个时代最新的制度、财富、教育和文化资源都由我们先享用，我们也享受了我们这个民族在家庭、学校和社会对下一代前所未有的宽容和关爱。

80 后艺术来了！我们还单纯，我们是纯色的一代，正在酝酿着这一代的人性和美学！

80 后代表艺术家将全面登场。

北京表情

附中时和同学在天安门前

在凤凰岭长城

Pure Generation

We are post-80s, the generation who are loved and highly valued by people. Due to cruel struggle for existence in the outer world and inner self, the modern intergenerational features of our whole nation scarcely break away from hatred and misery at various levels under the growth environment from family, school to society, but these intergenerational features on the post-80s seem to have disappeared overnight.

With the appearance of Super Girls, Liuxiang, Yaoming, Hanhan, etc. who are the idols of the post-80s, the art of the post-80s is following to appear. In view of probably causing ambiguity, we prefer to name the artists of post-80s with Pure Generation. Since China entered the modern world at the end of the 19th century, Chinese nation has scarcely possessed this collective generation features. The so-called Pure Generation refers to a series of open and social self-features which are occurring on them and has never been achieved in our nation for thousands of years, including relax, humor, confidence, acuity, loveliness, sex permissiveness and internationalization as well as self sense of reality brought by liberalization of information and transportation.

This is one of the important reasons why the post-80s deserve our love and value. Their art has appeared and showed a sign. The drawings, sculpture and Video art of the post-80s are less impacted directly by western vanguard art. What is most valuable is their artistic properties, as the intergenerational features of the whole post-80s, rarely have visual features such as suffering bitterly and having a deep hatred, self-sadness and dignifiedness. They rebuild the characters of the self of the new generation, including self-centeredness, grande illusion, game life, loveliness, etc, having a pure, upward and impactive power in vision.

This is one of the important reasons why the post-80s deserve our love and value. Their art has appeared and showed a sign. The drawings, sculpture and Video art of the post-80s are less impacted directly by western vanguard art. What is most valuable is their artistic properties, as the intergenerational features of the whole post-80s, rarely have visual features such as suffering bitterly and having a deep hatred, self-sadness and dignifiedness. They rebuild the characters of the self of the new generation, including self-centeredness, grande illusion, game life, loveliness, etc, having a pure, upward and impactive power in vision.

If comparing the intergeneration, the art of the previous generations almost finds its localization way during struggling and lingering between tradition continuance and western culture borrowing, but the localization mainly stays on the idea identities of symbols and political ideology and is hard to be normalized and sensationalized at empiricist level. The art of the post-80s is truly reflected at the levels of daily vision and self sensation. They seem to have easily gained the Chinese and contemporary image characteristics which the previous generations sought in vain. Thus, without a doubt, the local temperament and formal characteristics are the contemporary original self secretion in real sense.

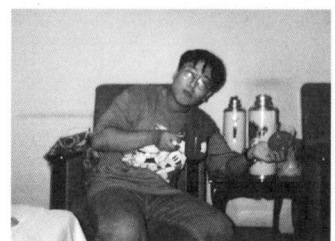

在附中的时候

The art of the post-80s shows the system experience and self-features in the super structure which is forming in China since the new century. Actually, the growth background of the post-80s has been reflected in Super Girls, Yaoming and Liuxiang. The Chinese Pop Music Idol Program—Super Girls in Hunan TV reveals that China has not only made transcendence in capital, labor mobility as well as production scale but also transcended America and other capitalist countries in the degrees of commercialization and entertainment of pop culture.

Compared with the previous generation, the literature and art of the post-70s also reflect the characteristics of this generation in the period of social transformation in China such as dignifiedness, reality, cruelty and self-centeredness. In the films directed by Jia Zhangke, the northern cities have experienced changes from county town, little town to modern city, which are not fully formed and are still in the interlacement of county town culture and city layout. In the stories written by Mianmian, the modern intellectual and elite culture from the west have been substituted by the rock, bars, young and cruel city life from the west as the same, which is just like the characters in the stories written by Haruki Murakami, who never care about truth and salvation of the world and others but begin to pay attention to self sensation and individual sensational destiny in pure youth, and who also have heredity of the previous generation and have been in the initial cruel process of realistic order collapse and social wealth extortion, such as moral injury of disordered society, cruelty to reality, self sense of frailty of urban indifference as well as hostility to social reality therefrom.

The post-80s happen to grow during Chinese reform and opening up and the rapid growth periods of economy, culture, life and so on. The society has completed the new super deconstruction period, people have been released from the past social structure and various concepts and consciousness gradually transform under new social formation, so there is no influence of accompanying newborn misery going down to this generation in the processes of breaking and transformation. The post-80s are mostly only child and are surrounded by favor from all aspects and orientation. Just because of this, we are amiable and lovely, friendly to others and the society and have a love for everything. The post-80s are safe from physical work and transition suffered by the previous generation because of well-off materials and social stability, therefore, most of them enter the spiritual road and liberation road transcending imagination. It is a new starting point of humanity progress of our nation and is also a self foundation of the post-80s surpassing the previous generation in art in reality.

We have enjoyed unprecedented openness, progress, materials, consumption, media and care. We can work and travel in another city by air or driving. Sometimes we participate in the talent shows of other provincial and civic broadcasting stations and may become well-known accidentally, thus becoming young stars and millionaires.

We are a generation full of dreams and happen to be born in an age we can realize the dreams.

In fact, the art of the post-80s really reflects the growth and self-features of this generation. Namely, the growth stage of the post-80s is mainly the 6 years of the new century, and at the stage, China has basically completed structural transformation and finally formed and will maintain the cultural features and institutional structure of androgynous society for quite a long period. From the beginning, the post-80s begin to enjoy lofty material life and spiritual life. Our surroundings are flooded with diverse new phenomena and new things dazzling us, including mobile phones, Internet, E-mail, credit cards, cash dispensers, bars, cultural park, 798 Art Factory, Songzhuang Art Park, etc. Due to expansion of universities, development of amusement culture, full-scale entry of Multinational Corporation, popularization of private cars, social media-control and star worship, etc. the difference between the material consumption and city utilities shortens locally, which facilitates the artists of the post-80s to open their angles of view to communicate with the cutting-edge art in the world and cooperate with the powerful gallery, so as to realize our artistic dreams in the maximum possibility.

Born in 1981, Fang Yixiu and Deng Yu both graduated from Guangzhou Academy of Fine Arts and drew roads, homuncule, trees, small animals, small furnitures, stars, moon and so on which are originated from their growth experience like key or puppet patterns of mobile phone's accessories are connected and arranged by various lines and reticular formation and put on the canvas background with diverse cool popular colors. Interestingly, the paint used by Deng Yu is not the special one but the nai polish in different colors. They just draw the pictures with cartoon image characteristics and the pictures are hard to be included in the scope of realistic ones, abstract ones or doodle drawing.

It is hard to say their drawings are for the sake of expressing certain sense and do not have new meanings. The grasp of patterns, hue and layout of the pictures mainly depends on self sensation, sentiment and growth experience in Guangzhou where the cartoon culture is popular in early period. Actually, they seldom have definite drawing technologies and skills, but it seems to be hard to grasp sometimes. These drawings are mainly types of soul secretion and have the characteristics of international cartoon culture, while, at the same time, it has difference from the cartoon drawing characteristics of Japan and America.

无题

The drawings of Shen Dapeng reflect the growth and characteristics of self portrait of the post-80s: red flag is still flying over the school, teachers with brief cases under their arms pass out of the school enclosure, a boy and a girl sit, seeming to have not suffered from life and social change but experienced exams. Their lovely but egoistic expression and cartoon T-shirt show a sense of innocence of having comfortable and wealthy lives and not caring anyone but also show a unique innocent power. Shen Dapeng was born in 1982 and graduated from Tianjin Academy of Fine Arts which is a college with level of drawing specialty ranking far lower, but his super painting realistically ability distinguishes him marvelously and is good in the eight great academies of Fine Arts and even in Europe and America.

平安梦

Indulging in the technical quality of languages and exquisite quality let the post-80s seem to have exceeded the painters in the previous generations. Another representative in this aspect is the WAZA group which graduated from Hubei Institute of Fine Arts and has 6 members in total. The members are all born around 1982 and 1983. Their 3D animated short film won the First Prize of Hangzhou International Anime Fair. The short film virtualized a length of TV talk show of American Singer, Michael Jackson who went to Wuhan for an interview and also virtualized a gibberish performance about local street culture of Wuhan by a little fan with Wuhan dialect on TV.

WAZA group depends on self study to grasp the 3D animation technology. Their artistic credo is that this generation shall attach importance to the technical quality of languages. In the age of electronic media, technology itself is a language. They are more conscious than other artists of post-80s in this point. Due to the shortening of local difference between electronic media and urban culture, in the places where the former artistic language falls behind and the cultural temperament appears countrified, such as Tianjin and Wuhan, the artistic works of Shen Dapeng and WAZA group have international language and image characteristics, which is a unique phenomenon of the art of post-80s.

在工作室和田宝明在一起

This generation grows in an age with highly developed physical environment and highest cultural diversity openness and internationalism. They enjoy more advantages of capitalism and socialism, making the post-80s have a sense of identity for China in renaissance and upward period from their hearts at the beginning. Irony and depreciation of China's realities in the art of previous generations seldom appear in their works.

Born in 1981 and graduated from Sichuan Fine Arts Institute, Gao Yu rebuilt the panda image with post-80 characteristics and reflected the spiritual metaphor. They grew under the red flag which is not a flag suffering from difficult years and being bullet-riddled in the battle but a flag flying in the wind and becoming red as cool as advertisement flag. They indulge in the virtual gory sensation, long for lover and love, face the reality with gloom and helplessness like internal affairs and admire Chinese traditional characteristics, etc. The drawings of Gao Yu have been given political and traditional titles but are almost cartooned by the play style of low and shallow images, for example, Losing Your Head and Shedding Blood expresses pretty panda heads dripping with blood and making a face; Death of Hermit portrays a lovely panda which died well under forest shadow with fresh wind dancing; Rich Culture Bloomed Brightly describes a symbol of cartoon saluting the tradition. Traditional burden and political cruelty are like psychic reality only related to "Symbol" 1 for the little pandas growing under the red flag.

The drawings of Guo Wen hail to the traditional landscapes. He appears more relaxed and intelligent compared to the great change to modern age by older generation painters to transform paintings. He changes the theme of landscape into "Hill Fire", makes the hilltop in the Chinese traditional landscape pictures burn with fire and lets fashionable men and women swimming in bikini and pants appear at the foot of the hill.
The sculpture of Jin Nv has sentimental and aesthetic visual style. She is more inclined towards young magic sentimental style. Her Grow up---Confusion is a sculpture of centaur. The upper body is a sad beautiful young girl who is a bit similar to that in the Japanese video games in model but sheds tears around her eyes and appears to be more vulnerable and easily-hurt than the video game girls who are always happy and in high morale. The lower half of the body is one leg stepping on the ground with feet and the other leg like a noble girl lifting a horse in the air gracefully. Jin Nv graduated from Sculpture Department, China Central Academy of Fine Arts and her sculpture reflects that the self spirit of this generation is a memory about fairy tales but not the enlightenment of the previous generation on revolution and myth

However, the post-80s seem to feel full of birth defects and unsatisfied, such as continuous study and exams, no longer having profound experiences brought by social instability and revolutionary changes, lightness of being and rich-poor polarization in affluent society. One drawing of Gao Yu's portrays that a large panda is abusing itself like a vacuous young man, pricking its eyes with knife and cutting off its own genitals. Born in 1981, Luo Dan is the son of Luo Zhongli, a famous painter. The oil painting of Luo Zhongli portrays a father tortured greatly and Luo Zhongli is honored as the image of a generation in China by criticism circle. But Luo Dan is determined to portray the grandson of this father as the image of post-80s who is singing rock music with microphone in hand in catharsis way. The grandson is not portrayed as a Bohemian young man in the sixties and seems to long for the revolution and passion lost in this generation.

The period since the new century can be called a China with Super Experience. The post-80s just grow in this period which our nation has never experienced for five thousand years. Although the adults in the previous generations experience this age at the same time, they bear historical bitter memories and responsibility burden while the post-80s do not. From the beginning, we grow in an age with a super structure of new formed economy and culture. They regale themselves on the latest systems, wealth, education and cultural resources in this age and we also regale ourselves on the unprecedented tolerance and care which our nation gives to the next generation in family, school and society.

The art of the post-80s is approaching! We are still pure, a pure generation are brewing humanity and aesthetics of this generation!

The representative artists of the post-80s are going to show fully.

飞翔的白羽毛

遗失的美好

李梦的艺术

李梦这次出版的作品,主要是 2007 年至 2008 年的作品,算顺应时代要求吧!一口气设计完,也很快就把这批作品搞出来了。从表象上看,是他去香港参加佳士得拍卖会,受东南亚当代艺术的影响,再说深点就是生理自然的选择,跟他个人的成长经历有关。

他受社会因素的影响可能很少,他的审美情趣和绘画手法,实质是非常个人化的手法。"卡通"艺术里的这一批人,都有一种神通的东西。卡通艺术,追根究底源于日本,小时候的变形金刚、花仙子等等,给他留下深刻印象。例如,变形金刚问世之后变成了国际共同语言,传达着正义感和友谊,充满着微笑,对他的创作影响很深。

这次出版的画传,大部分的作品属于少男少女系列,他借鉴了日本艺术家的设计元素,同时融入中国女孩的发型和服饰,让人看了感觉很轻松,很愉悦。在作品中,他尽量不用灰色,而选择用原色和各种间色的方式来表现,这可能跟他悲观的时间太长了有关,是灰到底点的时候的爆发。卡通里的大悲大喜场面在他作品里被去除,因为他认为少年永远是被期待的人群。这个阶段(2006 ~ 2008)的作品如果还延续用上面的方式去评论,好像就有点不太合适了,经过这些年的不断实验,他找到了自己的一些方法。然而,在此书的设计中难免加入了充数的作品,这些画,他自己也觉得有争议,有的作品甚至走进了一个死胡同里,拿出来展览就变成笑话了,可是他不拿出来做展览,就等于这个作品不存在!

1980 年是中国改革开放的第二年,就在这一年,李梦出生于辽宁省营口市。他对家乡的印象就是它并肩靠着大海!母亲河辽河和营口港,常常勾起他对家乡的思念和眷恋。

父母对他的美术启蒙教育影响并决定了他的人生美术之路。因为响应国家号召,家里只有他一个小孩,所以作为双职工的父母,生活虽然拮据,但李梦从小受到的可是非常好的正规美术基础教育。父亲是老三届的最后一届,经历过自然灾害、"文革"、89 动乱,在广州和海南当过水兵,转业回家后在公安系统做普通职工。虽说是公安系统,但他曾被部队指派到广州美术学院工作兵大学学习美术，目的是让艺术兵为部队服务。父亲转业回家后才有了李梦。从小父亲就对他很严厉，可能是很早年当兵经历有关。母亲是一个娴淑的女人，朴实、顾家，因为父亲在公安局上班比普通的工人每月多赚十几块钱，母亲就决定嫁给父亲，一过就是29年。

李梦最初是在营口创新小学读的书，启蒙老师陶红给予他很多关心，也鼓励他参加过很多美术比赛，虽然是不足一提的市级和省级比赛，但在当时还是让他感到十分激动。1996年，他到北京读中央工艺美院附中，开始正式接触美术基础教育。在附中上学期间，他碰到了两位好老师，文化课导师丁淑英和专业导师马晓光，这两位老师在教学方面都极其的负责，每个星期都要求学生画15张速写，实在没什么可画的，就跑到北京站去画游客和民工。那时北京站管理不是很严格，经常有学生去那画速写，因为经济原因，晚上画好后没车回家，就跟那些游客民工呆一宿，现在想起来还是蛮开心的。在附中的三年是他在学生时代最开心的三年，也是最艰辛的三年。附中的美术教育可以说是相当正规的，石膏切面像、石膏头、石膏半身像、人物头骨、扒皮人、人物头像、胸像、半身像、泳装，一切都是正规的即很有程序的美学教育，其中还有中外美术史和美学基础教育。他们本着"想要出人头地，就得背后遭罪"的思想，努力奋斗。同学和老师的努力方向就是让同学们学习感性教育，当时是没有物理和化学课程的，数学课程也很少，大部分的时间就是施行整体美术基础教学。

1999年李梦以全国5个设计专业总分第一的专业名次考入当时的天津科技大学环境艺术设计专业。因为英语的原因，没能进中央美术学院，这成为了他的一大遗憾。其实听起来环境艺术设计跟架上美术关系不大，可能是因为设计的东西要求理性的东西多一点吧，之后他放弃了设计，回到纯美术道路上，他的这一选择可能是跟商业现实有关。有的人为了艺术，而李梦首先考虑经济，第二才是艺术。

在学院上课，教学是重点。一方面老师希望你受特别传统、特别严格的训练；一方面自己又找不到方向。那时候严重到可以把老师关在门外面，比方老师有一个月的课，过了两个星期，连教室都进不来，学生把门锁上，老师在外面敲门，大家就放王力宏的歌，放的声音很大，假装听不见，于是就把老师气坏了，谁碰到这种情况也不愿来上课，时间长了就变成放任自流了。在学院的这段时间里，主要是去看展览，天津和北京经常跑。看美术馆，呆图书馆，看画册，同学之间喝酒聊天，等到了千禧年——2000年，当时感觉到，再大的世界，总得有个地儿是你呆的地方，是你立脚的地方，那怎么办呢？就回到原始状态，用6B铅笔起稿，然后慢慢到5B、4B……一直到6H，等于说，从最原始的状态再往前进行。

传统大学的生活积极乐观，五湖四海的同学汇聚到一起，虽有很多矛盾，但更多的是值得回忆的故事。术学院院长张品在毕业设计的时候就给了他很多的帮助。

李梦开始了解中国当代艺术就是到中央美术学院附中看见刘小东先生，当时他还是美院附中的一名普通教师。他当时的一些重要作品是《笑话》、《张元向宁岱求婚》、《打哈欠的男人体》、《白头到老》等。在考学的压力下他觉得刘小东先生的画很好，但只是知道好，后来在大学之后才体味到在当时刘小东先生的作品在技术方面学习了弗洛伊德的色彩方法，摒弃了苏派的马克西莫夫和列宾的前辈学院派基础美术教育。弗洛伊德似乎是悲哀的，一辈子在室内画一些大人体和肉体，而刘小东先生却把中国的当代艺术观点和思维继承并发展了弗罗伊德的美术，可以随意的画他自己喜欢的内容，既得到学院派的认可，又得到所谓"江湖"画家的普遍好评。东北的山水并不算美，一般的画家都把艺术方向寄情于人，对于人性和亲情的表达。他很喜欢的画家还有申玲、龙力游、宫力龙、夏俊娜、喻红等。所以现在看当时这一类画家的画，还是很激动的。

本世纪初，以高举玩世现实主义的大旗的当代艺术家如雨后春笋一样涌现。代表人物当属方力钧、刘炜、岳敏钧、杨少斌等人。

可能是由于生活的艰辛或者是对艺术的不断追求当代艺术，也伴随着改革开放的号角如火如荼的发展这些当代艺术家张扬个性，以一种幽默和调侃的方式展示自我个性，尽量脱离学院派的框架束缚，有的艺术甚至发展成含有色、暴力、政治等因素的方式。

本世纪初，放眼于东南亚艺术，当属日本的当代艺术值得我们关注，李梦也正是怀着和平友谊的态度去看待日本当代艺术。

可能是受二战战败的心理影响，日本艺术家的作品大都颜色比较鲜亮，饱和度高。村上隆的作品，似乎预示着国际化卡通一代的到来。草间弥生的布面丙烯南瓜系列，奈良美智的《和平》，年轻一些的松浦浩之和80后艺术家长泽郁美，都把卡通艺术的形式推进到一个新的艺术高度。他们作为新一代艺术家，已经不属于关上门搞艺术的年代。他们开始关注社会现实，从复杂的社会生活中简化问题。有的还认为重要的不是艺术，经济第一，文化第二，艺术第三，这与父母辈吃苦太多有关。艺术家先考虑的是填饱肚子的问题，生活改善后，开始考虑作品的文化性。而到新的高度，年轻一代会慢慢体味艺术的社会性，哲学性，思想性，政治性，媒体责任感。前辈艺术家往往关注美好的艺术，比如说，女性美，风景，静物，朋友之间的友谊，或者放言之军民雨水情等。而新一代艺术家的进步思想开始涌现，反映社会现实、无奈、抑郁、悲哀、教育、环境保护、政治腐败等。激进的艺术家把心中的喜悦和不满抽象化，用各种绘画形式表达。比如说石心宁、苍鑫、马六明等。70后当代艺术家中，非常好的也很多，比如说张小涛、管勇、李继开、陈可、高禹、徐毛毛等。

说到自己的艺术，李梦认为比较独特，似乎反映着艺术家以理性反思的眼光重新审视当代。经济和文化的全球化到来，促使21世纪的中国经济持续高速发展，各种文化，新知识涌入，中国进入一种所谓的"社会变迁"或"社会转型"之时，它具体并直接地表现为经济体制、社会结构、文化模式、价值观念等各个领域的深刻变化。这一切对固有的传统提出了挑战，也是对于人们原已形成的社会心理系统形成巨大的冲击，这是一个回归本我的时代。精神模式、价值观念、人与世界的关系、艺术趣味、艺术与社会的关系等等，皆会发生一系列的精神反思。

作为当今中国社会之主体的人，他们正身临其境，自身势必受其影响，并微妙地在发生着变化。中国，与西方世界相似，产生了一个具有鲜明中国特色的庞大群体——他们个性独立，自我意识强烈：分布在社会各个

附中采风和同学们的合影

和同学们在一起

和张东红在一起

领域，皆有着突出的成就；物质生活无虑，懂得享受精神生活；重视生活的品位。他们的要求与观念等，激发并改变着中国社会经济文化及各个方面的发展，并产生着巨大的影响。李梦成长于改革开放的年代，感受着当代一股多元而自由的风气，他既处于中心又游离于边缘，既反思一切又试图去续写一切。

面对中国经济的快速发展，消费文化的蔓延与盛行，面对人们日益沉浸于一种过高想象的迷幻享乐主义，他却静下心来对当代问题进行反思，以反叛甚至玩世不恭的态度质疑并反思着一切，如中国传统教育体制，意识形态等。他在文化的深层游荡，强调着个体的独立性、主体性与价值性，强调着中国新的社会阶层，精英所应具有的思想、角色、价值观与责任感。他已不仅仅是一种富足的存在，他应有自己的历史责任感与精神象征性。也许在某种程度上，他是中国当代发展轨道上不停歇的导向者，他对社会更重要的意义是引领和维护。这样一种中国当代社会文化现象，在视觉艺术领域里，与其相伴而生，给予艺术呈现的似乎就深深体现在他的艺术中。他看似是在社会的边缘"消解崇高"，却又似在社会的中心试图去"树立崇高"。

他的艺术有着一种强烈的情境性和叙事性特征。在空旷而深沉的画面背景前，卡通人物戏剧性地在展示着某一时刻凝固的状态，他们或放纵想象，或沉醉沉思，或激烈辩论，或翘首期盼，以严肃而又带有些讽刺的语调质疑现实，以审视的视角强调个体。这些场景，既似荒诞不经，又似直指现实；即严谨有序，又恢宏博大，气宇轩昂。谈到这些作品，我们没有感到娱乐，而更多的是一种忧郁、感伤、沉重、反醒，他试图让大家沉浸在每一个画面的场景中，与画中每一个人物对话交流之时的那种迷惘、省思、沉重与责任，更加触动着我们的心灵。人的一种独立性、主题性、价值性，存在的一种责任感与自我精神象征性，跃然于画面之上，他对这个时代中的人，以及那些新的社会阶层的现状与存在迹象及思考，亦渗透其中。

为了突出表达自己的这种艺术主题与创作理念，他在不断的探索中找到了一种专属于自己的独特的个人创造性语汇特征，而这些艺术表现语汇特征，可以说渗透着专属于中国文化意义上的特别符号内涵，由此更回应展现着艺术家所处国度、民族及时代的当下性问题的思考。

　　首先，最近作品中的人物，大概分两个系列，小女孩的天真，对美好生活的向往和小男孩胸怀志气。同时变形金刚所展现出来的正义感，给孤独的人带来各种联想，带来我们同年的回忆。可以看出，色彩以单纯的粉色、红色、蓝色等为主，富有强烈独特的中国文化象征意义和审美品格，强化了艺术家对当代中国及中国人的关注思考。当然，他一直是非常强调画面色彩对视觉感觉上的刺激和震撼，这从某种程度上说也许更映射出现代人生活节奏对生活方式和观念对艺术领域、审美的影响，因为当代人在审美理想上追求视觉的冲击力，心灵的震撼力。所以，在他的艺术中，他选用了蕴涵特定意义及当代审美的色彩，创造出独具个人语言特征的人物形象造型，从而形成了他自己鲜明而强烈的个人艺术面貌。这些直观且略带些符号化特征的形象及鲜亮刺目的色彩，突出了他作品的风格。但是，当我们一幅幅作品细细看来，每一个人物或者变形金刚又有着丰富的变化。这些表情呈现无奈、忧郁、迷惘，是当下消费文化极其享乐主义带给人们的一种过度虚妄想象的快乐感觉的显现。这预示了当代人们日益追求物质化和娱乐化的过程中，产生着一种危机，这种危机，不仅体现在人们在精神上缺少的依靠与寄托，也体现在个人主体性价值的反思与追问。多元时代及中国社会转型期给予当代人的这些影响，深深体现在李梦的艺术中，他将对时代的思考植入到自己的艺术中。

Li Meng's Art

The works published this time of Li Meng are mostly works of years 2007 and 2008, which can be seen as adapting to the requirements of the times- designed at a stretch and then published immediately. Viewed from state, this batch of works show the influence he attended Christie's in Hong Kong and saw contemporary art in South-east Asia; besides, the works are deep in the selection of physiological nature, which are also affected by his personal growth. The works might be little influenced by social elements for "personal feeling of beauty and painting techniques" is very individual skills substantively. There is something like theurgist in art of "cartoon". Cartoon art derives from Japan actually as Transformers and Hana no ko lunlun, etc., which impressed him a lot when he was still young. Transformers became common international language to transmit feeling of justice as well as friendships, thereby filling with smiling. Actually mostly works published this time are aiming at boys and girls; thereinto, Li Meng borrowed Japan artists' design elements for reference and blended into hair styles and fineries element of Chinese girls, so the works makes people feeling more relax and joyful.

In the works, gray is rarely selected but using primary color and various secondary colors for showing, which may because the author was gloomy for too long and is the break out. We still remembered the colors in Final Fantasy full of imagination and hope. Scenes with mingled feeling were wiped off in his works. Youngsters are expected forever. During this period, namely years of 2006 and 2007, until 2008, the present works of Li Meng actually still use the said method; he found some personal methods through uninterrupted experiments in these years. Dummy works are unavoidable in designing, which are controversial even thought by himself once painted out; some works are formalist and he won't take them out for exhibition for once exhibited, they might become jokes, however, if he doesn't take them out for exhibition, that means the works are inexistence!

Li Meng was born in Yingkou city, Liaoning province in 1980- the second year since Chinese Reform and Opening Up. His impression on his hometown is namely leaving to the sea!, Liaohe River, Mother River, and Yingkou Port are his missing and reminiscence to hometown.

Formative education of art from his parents influences and determines his lifetime road of art. At that time, for the purpose of responding for national appeals, his parents, both employees, gave him, the only child in his family, the conditions to receive normal basic art education since he was still young although their life is not rich. His father was the last term in Lao Sanjie, who suffered from natural disasters, Cultural Revolution, 1989 Tiananmen Square massacre and was a bluejacket once in Guangzhou and Hainan; after demobilization and return hometown, he was a common employee in public security system. Although worked in public security system, his father was once sent to university for workers, peasants and soldiers, Guangzhou Academy of Fine Arts for learning art, so as to serve for army as an art soldier. Li Meng was born after the demobilization of his father. His father was strict on him, which might be related with his former soldier experience; his mother is a ladylike woman, simple and homely. Only because of the additional dozen Yuan each month his father earned in Public Security Bureau than common workers, his mother decided to marry with his father and up to now, they have been lived for 29 years. Li Meng studied in Chuangxin Primary School in Yingkou and his first teacher Tao Hong, gave him much care; he participated in many art competitions which, although not competitions with grade of city and provincial, made him exciting at that time!

北京表情

In 1996, Li Meng came to Beijing and studied in China Central Arts & Crafts Institute Attached Middle School and formally touched with basic education of art. At that time, the education there was really very: both Ding Shuying, the tutor of cultural course, and Ma Xiaoguang, the professional instructor, are most responsible teachers in China! He had to draw 15 pictures of quick sketch every week. Sometimes he didn't know what to draw; he would run to Beijing station to draw tourists and workers, ha-ha! At that time, the management of Beijing station was not very strict and many students came there for quick sketching. Due to economic reason, sometimes he drew at night and there was no bus for return; he would stay there for one night; fellows there went on well with him although different body smells emerged. Ha-ha! It was enjoyable even when thinking of that nowadays. Three years in Attached Middle School was the happiest three years, but also most hardly; art education in Attached Middle School can be said very formal: all are very formal including plaster section image, plaster head, plaster bust, character skull, scalping person, character head image, bust, half-length and swimsuit, namely Aesthetics education with approval program; there were also educations of history of art in China and foreign countries and basic education of Aesthetics. Once you want to get advanced in the society, you have to suffer more rearwards. The aim that students and teachers make effort was that enabling students to study perceptual education; courses of physics and chemistry were not available at that time, and math course was few also. Mostly students were implementing entire art basic education.

In 1999, Li Meng entered the specialty of environmental art of Tianjin University of Light Industry with five number ones in five design specialties of the country. Because of English, he didn't get into China Central Academy of Fine Arts, which is still a pity until now. It seems that environmental art design is not closely related to easel art: something to be designed requires more in rationality; therefore, he then abandoned design and returned to pure art, which might be related to commerce. Some people are for art, but Li Meng considers economy firstly, and then art.

The lesson in the university was represented in teaching: from one aspect, the teacher hoped you to receive very traditional and strict training; from the other aspect, they were failed to find correct directions. At that time, even teacher could be excluded outside the classroom; for example, if a teacher had a course for one month, two weeks later, he/she even couldn't come into the classroom! Student locked the door, teacher was knocking on the door, students would play songs of Wang Lihong, etc., with a huge volume and pretended couldn't hear outside, which angered the teacher deeply; if you are encountered this situation, you would not come as well. Long time later, students became easy and would mostly come to exhibition and run between Tianjin and Beijing, visit art museum, read in library, read painting album, drink and chat with classmates; then in 2000, at that time you felt that: there must be a place for you in such a huge world, but what shall we do? Then back to original status. Starting with 6B pencil, and then slowly turned to 5B, 4B, etc. until 6H; that's to say that when you are up to another stage, the starting point is to return to the original status, and then go forward from the original status.

Traditional life in university is positive and optimistic, classmates from all corners of the land gathered together with much illogicality, but more stories worthy to be remembered. Zhang Pin, dean of art institute, gave him much help during his graduation design.

The moment Li Meng began to know Chinese Contemporary Art was started when he meeting with Liu Xiaodong in China Central Academy of Middle School; at that time, Liu Xiaodong was still a common teacher in Attached Middle School. Li Meng felt good if just talking about some important works of Liu Xiaodong at that time like Joke, Zhang Yuan proposes to Ning Dai yawning man body, lifelong happiness, etc. under the pressure of examination, but only good; later after entering the university Li Meng experienced that Liu Xiaodong at that time studied the color method of Floyd in technical aspect and abandoned academism basic art education in Soviet style from father of Maksimov and Repin in his works. Floyd seems woeful, he drew some huge human body and inside for his life time; however, Liu Xiaodong inherited the points of view and thoughts of Chinese Contemporary Art as well as developed art of Floyd, and could draw contents he likes at will, who was not only recognized by academism, but also been well judged by so-called "around" drawers. Landscapes of Northeast isn't beautiful, general drawers will express their art feeling through person and the expression on humanity and relationship. Drawers I liked very much also include Shen Ling, Long Liyou, Gong Lilong, Xia Junna, Yu Hong, etc. therefore, I am still exciting when watching these painter's paintings until now. At the beginning of this century, contemporary artists highly holding flags of performing realism were emerged one by one, representatives including Fang Lijun, Liu Wei, Yue Minjun, Yang Shaobin, etc.!

It may because of hardness of life or uninterrupted pursuance in art. Contemporary Art, accompanied with Reform and Opening up, was developed in full swing. These contemporary artist stinked individual characters, shown personal selfhood in a humorous and kidding way, and tried to get away from frame bondage from academism. Some art methods were even developed into something including eroticism, violence and polity.

At the beginning of this century, contemporary art of Japan was of course most worthy to be concentrated when scanning widely on art of Southeast Asia. He saw Japanese Contemporary Art with an attitude with peace and friendship also. It may be influenced by psychology of defeat in World War II, most works of Japanese artists had bright colors with high saturation.

Works of Murakami seemed to predict the coming of international cartoon era! Pumpkin series with propylene cloth cover of Kusama, Peace of Nara, younger including Hiroyuki Matsuura and 80 after generation artist, Ikumi Nagasawa promoted style of carton art into a new art degree!

As artists of a new era, it is not a time of researching art by closing the door any longer. He began to care about social reality and simplify problems from complex social life. Some still considered that art were not the most important, economy the first, culture the second, and art the third; this is related to too much hardness in parents' generation. The first problem artists considered is cram themselves, after better life, they began to think about culture of works. Then reaching to a new degree, the new generation will slowly experience sociality, philosophy, ideological content, political character, and media responsibility of art. Fore artists tend to focus beautiful art, for example, female

与程晓、李伟在一起

附中采风与老师、同学们在一起

charm, landscape, still objects, friendships between friends, or deep relationships between army and civilians, etc. Progressive thinking of artists of a new generation begun to emerge, which reflects social reality, helpless, blues, sadness, education, environmental protection, misgovernment, etc. Jacobinical artists abstracted their happiness and unsatisfactory inner heart, and then expressed in various painting styles. Artists including Shi Xinning, Cang Xin, Ma Liuming, etc. There are many good 70 after generation artists as well, for example, Zhang Xiaotao, Guan Yong, Li Jikai, Chen Ke, Gao Yu, Xu Maomao, etc.

As for his own art, Li Meng considered it was unique; it seemed that artists review the contemporary era with an eye of sense and reflection. The arrival of economic and cultural globalization urged the economy in China in 21 century to rapidly developed; various cultures, new technologies and consultations swarmed, China entered into a so-called a time of "social change" and "society transformation"; it was concretely and directly reflected as deeply changes in various regions including economical systems, social structures, cultural modes, value concepts, etc. All these brought forward challenges to immanent tradition and impact greatly on social psychology system which was originally formatted among people; it will be an era with a series of spiritual reflection and oneself return in spiritual mode, value concept, relation between human and the world, art interests, relation between art and society, etc.

As main body of Chinese society nowadays, people are now experiencing personally and would be influenced as well as changed delicately. Be similar to western world, a huge group with bright Chinese characteristics appears in China,, who has individual characteristics and strong self-consciousness and is distributed in various regions of the society with outstanding achievements, secure material living, understand how to enjoy spiritual life, focuses on life quality, etc.; their requirements and ideas are cultivating and altering cultures of Chinese society and economy as well as development in various aspects, and generate huge influences. It seems like a new era belonging to us.
He was growing in an era of Reform and Opening-up and sensing about the trend of contemporary multi-element and freedom. He not only is the center but also.

Facing with the rapid development of Chinese economy, the spread and popularity of consumer culture and watching people immersing in a magic hedonism with over standard imagination, however, he calmed down and reflected on contemporary problems, oppugned and reflected the overall with, such as Chinese traditional education system and ideology, etc., with revolt and even cynicism. He wanders deeply in society and culture, emphasizes the individuality, subjectivity and valuable of individual, stresses ideas, characters, values and responsibility of elites in new social hierarchy in China; he is not only a rich existence, but also he shall have his own historical responsibility and spiritual symbolism. Maybe from some aspect, he is a tireless guide on Chinese contemporary developing track; moreover, the more important meaning he played to the society is guidance and maintenance.

In the field of visual arts, such a phenomenon of Chinese contemporary social culture, generated along with visual arts and emerged as art, was deeply shown in his art. He seems "clearing up loftiness" at edge of the society, but also tries to "building loftiness" in the middle of society.

His art has a characteristic of strong situation and Narrative. In front of the background with picture open but dark, carton characters are dramatically showing a caky state at a very moment; they are indulgently imagining, or deeply thinking, or incisively arguing, or looking forward, questioning the reality with serious but acid tones and stressing individuals from different aspects.

These scenes looked like preposterous, but they directly reflected the reality, thereby being not only with order and discipline, but also being spectacular and extensive as well as grand and solemn. When talking about these works, we didn't sense enjoyment, but more are a kind of feeling, as gloomy, sentiment, heavy and reflection. He tries to immerse everyone into the scene of each picture; when communicating with every character in the picture, a sense of maze, meditation, heavy and responsibility, further touches our hearts. Human individuality, theme, value, a responsibility of existence and self-spiritual symbol appear vividly in the picture. He also adds in current situations as well as existence evidence and thought of people from this era, namely these new social hierarchies.

In order to outstandingly express his art theme and creative concept, he found a unique individual creative vocabulary characteristic specially belonging to himself during continuous exploration. It can be said that these art representing vocabulary characteristics are enriched with special symbol meaning socially belonging to Chinese cultural sense, and therefore further react and show thinking on contemporary problems in country, nation, and era artists are living.

Firstly, characters in recent works are probably divided into two series: girls with puerility and yearn toward beautiful life; and boys determined with transformers full of justice and bring loners with various imagination and our memories to childhood.

It can be seen that the application of simple colors like pure pink, red and blue is full of strong and unique Chinese cultural symbolic meaning and aesthetic quality and strengthens the concentration and consideration on contemporary China and Chinese of artists. Of course, he has been greatly stressed on the picture color all long to bring people a stimulation and convulsion in vision and sense; this, at some extent., may further reflect the influence on art field and aesthetic appreciation from the life rhythm, living style and concept of modern people, since contemporary people are looking for impact in vision and convulsion in soul on ideality of aesthetic appreciation.

Therefore, in his art, he selected colors containing specific meanings and contemporary aesthetic appreciation and created character imagine sculpt with unique individual language characteristics, so as to form bright and strong personal art appearance of his own. These direct characters with slight symbolic characteristics and bright colors stand out styles of his works. However, when we are appreciating his works carefully with one picture after another, every character or transformer has rich changes. These face expressions have helpless, gloomy and maze, and also bring people a happy feeling with over standard imagination under such a society of lack of consume culture with huge hedonism. This predicts that a crisis is generated during the process of contemporary people looking for material and entertainment; this crisis is not only embodied that people are lack of depending and bailment in spirit, but also is incarnated in reflection and closely question of personal principle value. Multi-element era and Chinese society transitional period brought contemporary people these influence, deeply embodied in his art and set considerations of era into his art.

LIMENG
李梦

WORKS
作品

志气男孩／AMBITION BOY／布面丙烯／90cm×60cm／2008年

守蓝色的梦/BLUE DREAM/布面丙烯/100cm×80cm/2008年

棒球男孩／BASEBALL BOY／布面丙烯／90cm×60cm／2008年

高尔夫男孩／GOLF BOY／布面丙烯／90cm×60cm／2008年

北京之恋／LOVE IN BEIJING／布面丙烯／90cm×60cm／2008年

马面生活／TWO SIDES LIFE／布面丙烯／100cm×80cm／2008年

♪无所依／A BOY HAVE NO DEPEND ON／布面丙烯／60cm×90cm／2008年　（P40～P41）

偏激的男孩／EXTREME BOY／布面丙烯／100cm×100cm／2008年

忧郁中的男孩／A BOY IN DEPRESSION／布面丙烯／100cm×100cm／2008年
友谊历久一样浓／FRIENDSHIP CHANGE TO DENSE DAY BY DAY／布面丙烯／100cm×100cm／2008年　(P44～P45)

梦见铁达尼／DREAM FOR TITANIC／布面丙烯／60cm×50cm／2008年

知道/I KNOW/布面丙烯/60cm×50cm/2008年

红果／RED FRUIT／布面丙烯／130cm×180cm／2008年　(P49～P50)

表情二／BEIJING EXPRESSION 2／布面丙烯／130cm×180cm／2008年　（P52～P53）

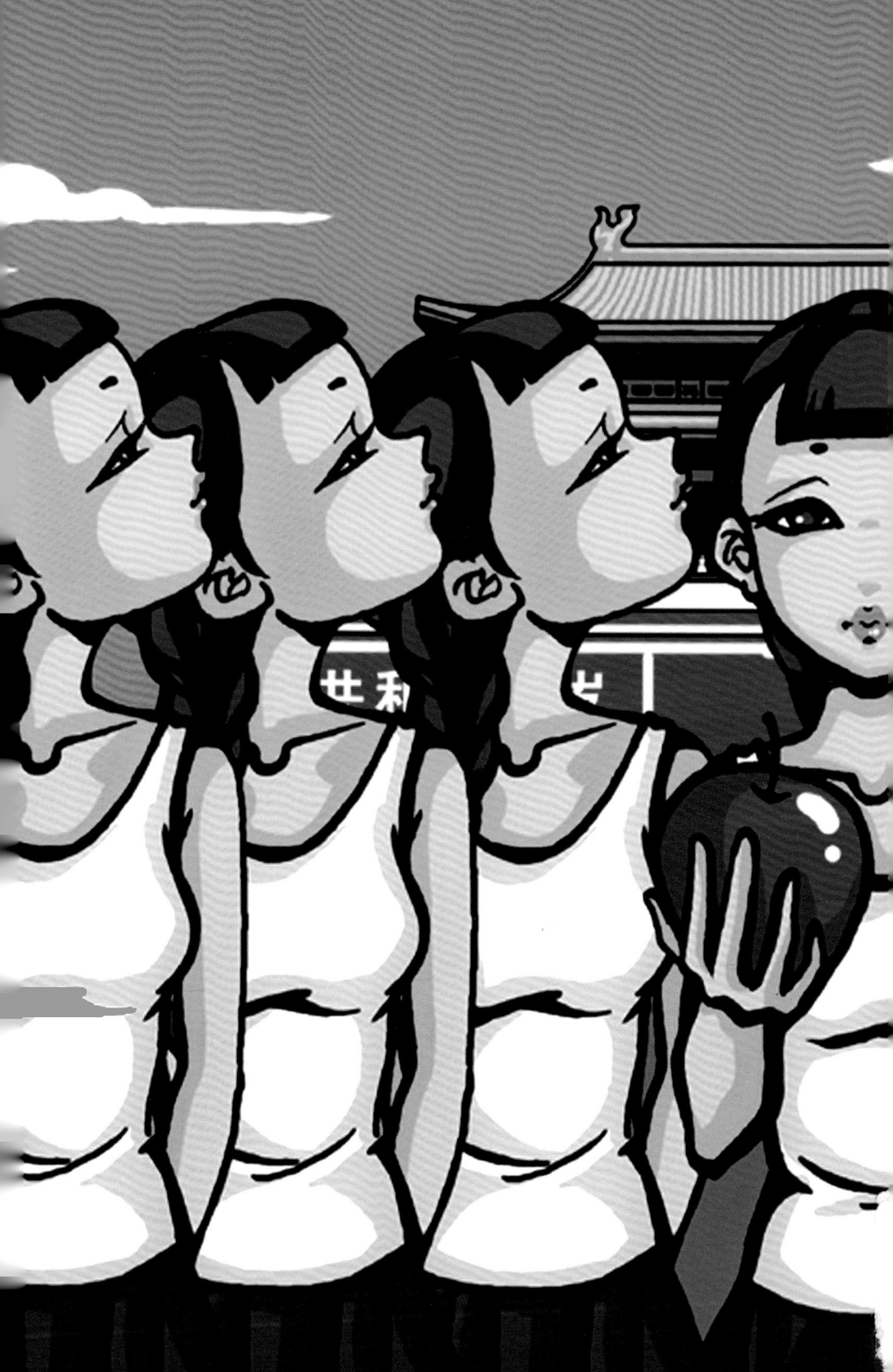

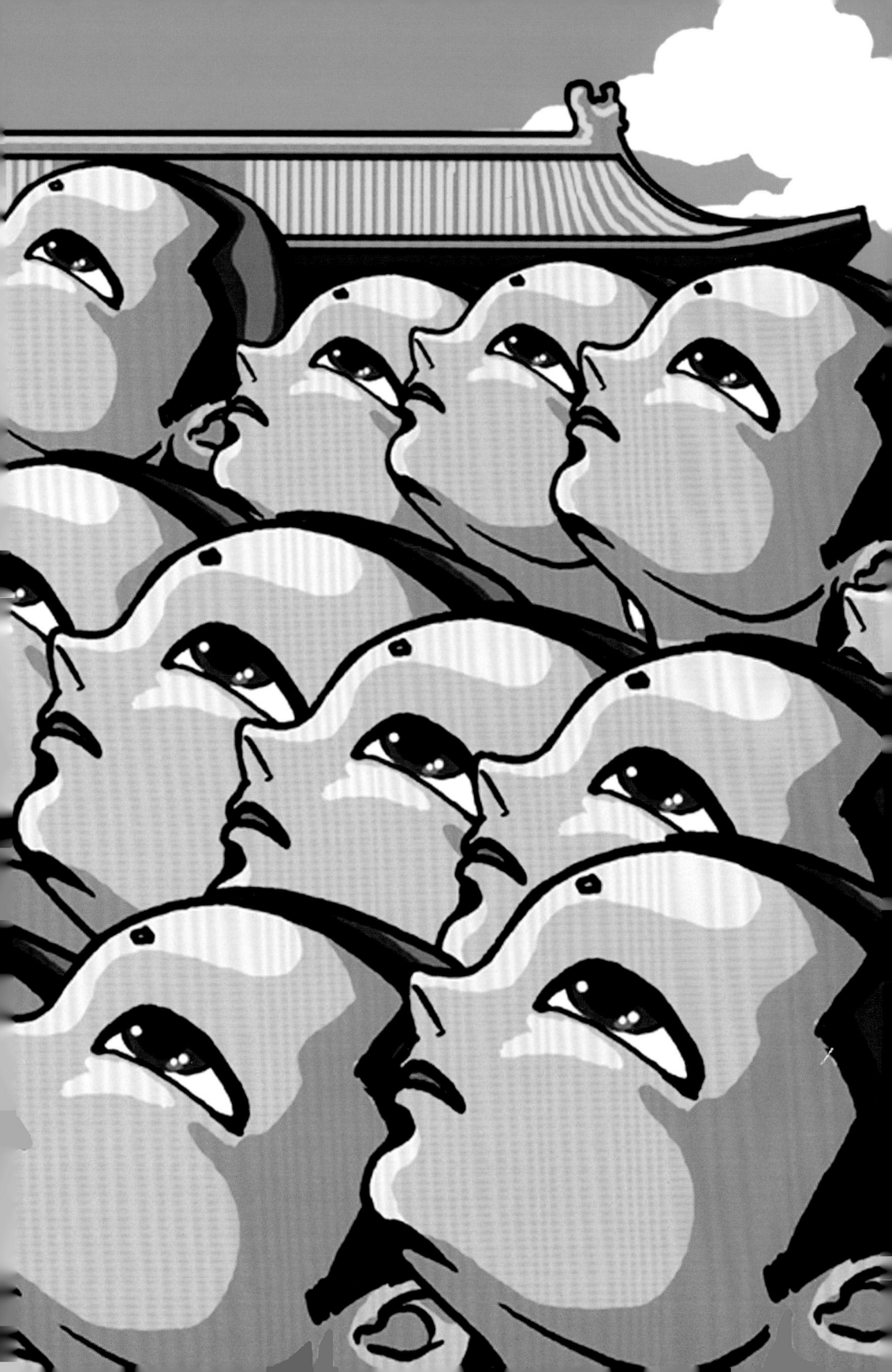

天安门前的标准动作二/STANDARD MOVEMENTS IN THE TIANANMEN SQUARE 2/布面丙烯/180cm×130cm/2008年

闲云野鹤／FERR TRAVEL IN TIANANMEN SQUARE／布面丙烯／180cm×130cm／2008年

天安门前的标准动作／STANDARD MOVEMENTS IN THE TIANANMEN SQUARE／布面丙烯／180cm×130cm／2008年

美丽的天安门/BEAUTIFUL TIANANMEN SQUARE/布面丙烯/180cm×130cm/2008年
北京表情/BEIJING EXPRESSION/布面丙烯/130cm×180cm/2008年　(P58~P59)

天使在你心中／ANGEL IN YOU HEART／布面丙烯／180cm×130cm／2008年

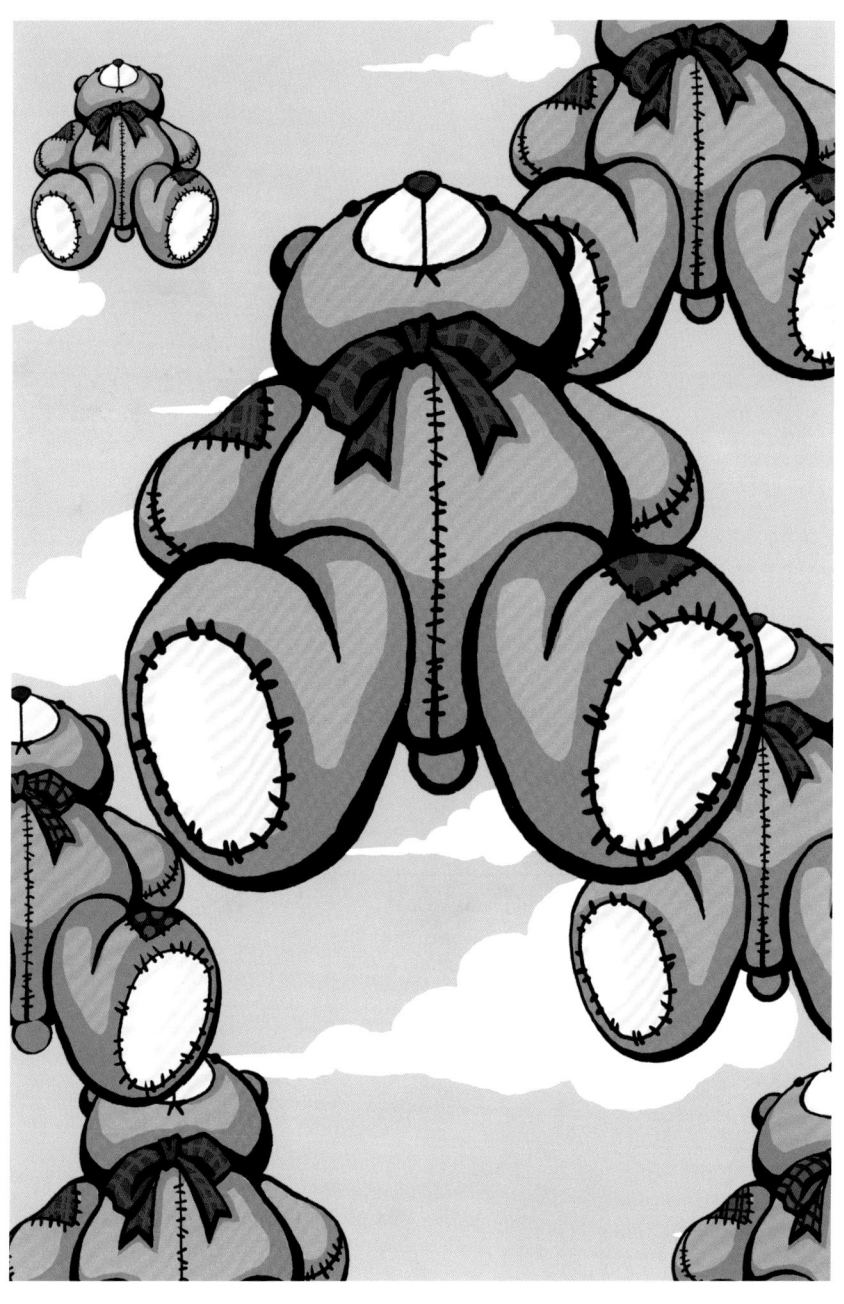

玩具熊礼物/TOY BEAR PRESENT/布面丙烯/180cm×130cm/2008年

微风中的女孩/GIRL IN BREEZE/布面丙烯/100cm×80cm/2008年

青春故事／YOUTH STORY／布面丙烯／100cm×80cm／2008年

飞翔的白羽毛/FIY.FLY/布面丙烯/100cm×100cm/2008年
矛盾中的男孩/A BOY IN CONTRADICTION/布面丙烯/100cm×100cm/2008年

青春故事2／YOUTH STORY 2／布面丙烯／90cm×60cm／2008年

分手快乐／HAPPY AFTER SAY GOOD-BYE／布面丙烯／90cm×60cm／2008年

亭爱的女孩／WAITING GIRL／布面丙烯／100cm×80cm／2008年

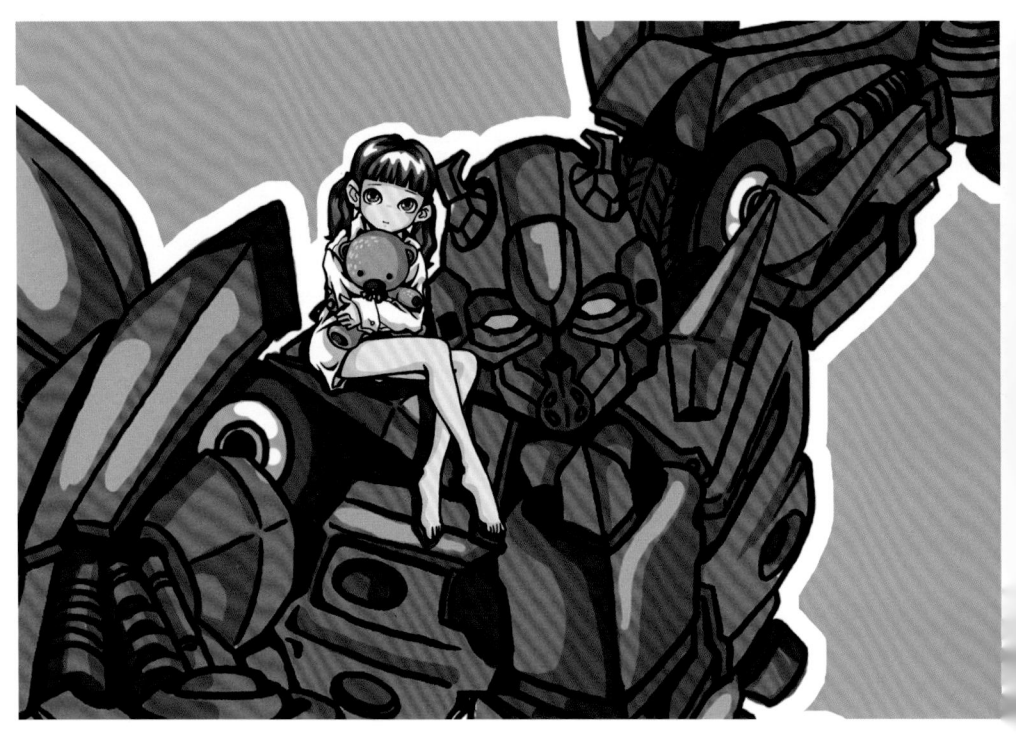

守护神3/PATRON SAINT 3/布面丙烯/130cm×180cm/2008年 （P69～P70）

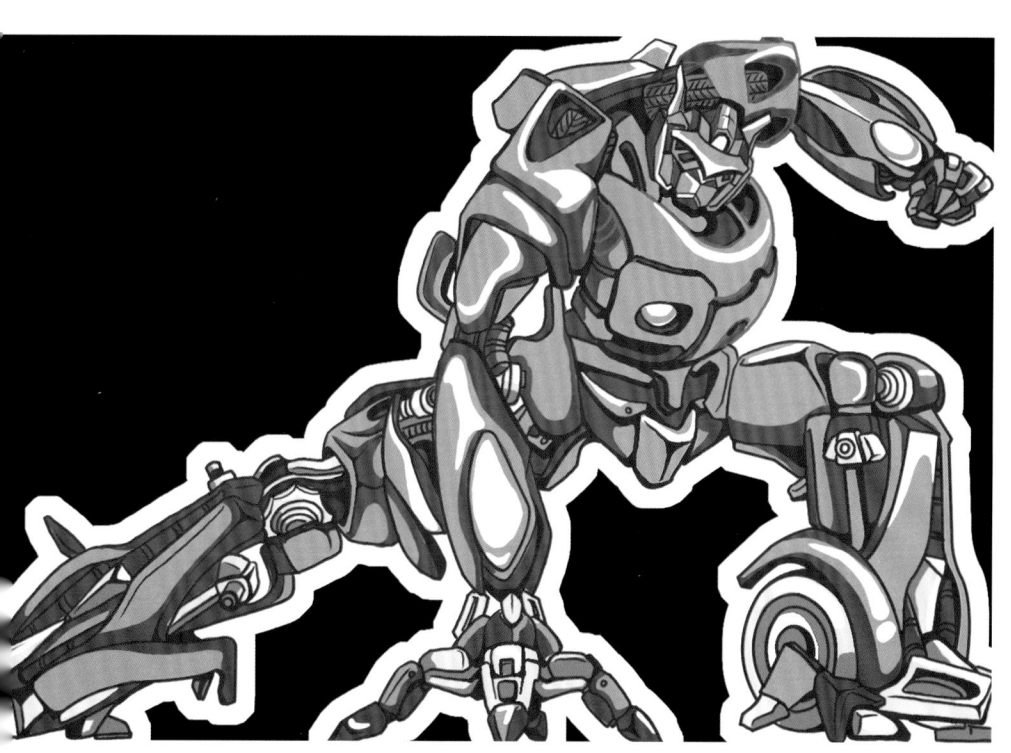

神4/PATRON SAINT 4/布面丙烯/130cm×180cm/2008年　(P72～P73)

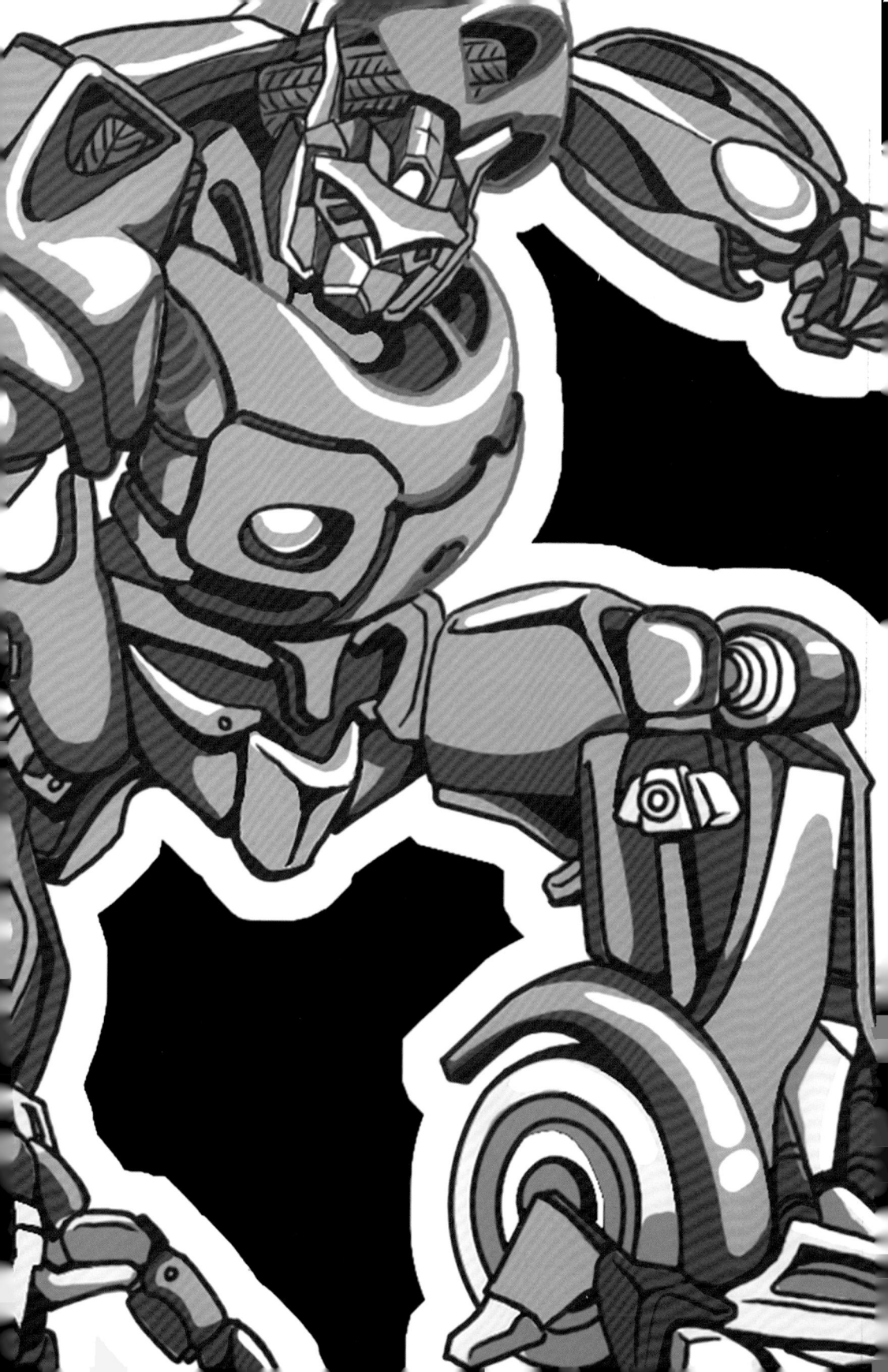

擎天柱/QINGTIANZHU/布面丙烯/180cm×130cm/2008年
守护神1/PATRON SAINT 1/布面丙烯/180cm×130cm/2008年

力士3/MUSCLEMAN 3/布面丙烯/180cm×130cm/2008年

士1/MUSCLEMAN 1/布面丙烯/180cm×130cm/2008年

力士2／MUSCLEMAN 2／布面丙烯／180cm×130cm／2008年

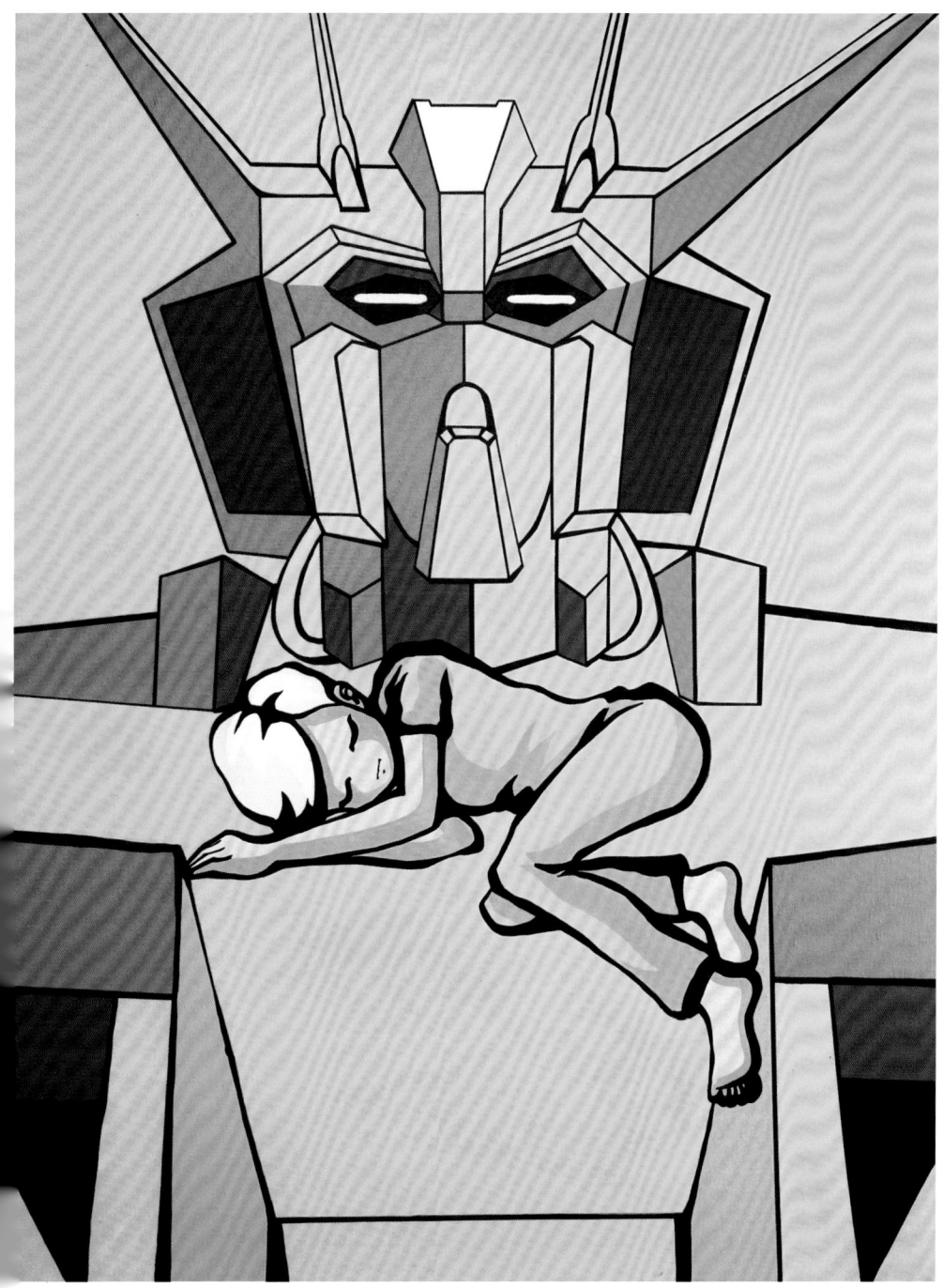

上 安梦／WELL DREAM／布面丙烯／150cm×120cm／2008年

冬天柱／QINGTIANZHU／布面丙烯／130cm×180cm／2008年 （P80～P81）

乐园中的女孩／GIRL IN PARADISE／布面丙烯／60cm×50cm／2008年

甘言蜜语/SWEET LANGUAGE/布面丙烯/60cm×50cm/2008年

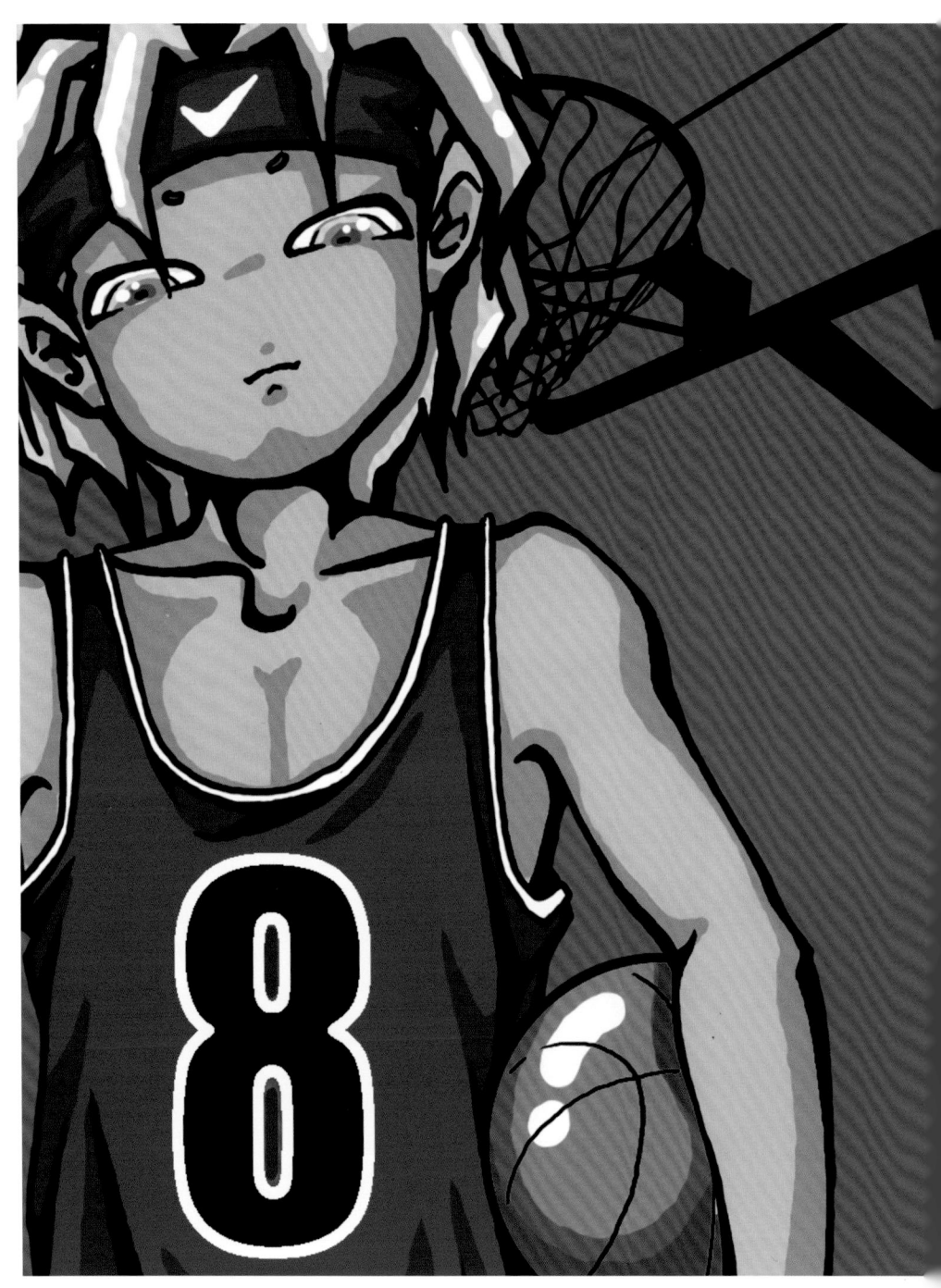

寄情于篮球的男孩/BASKETBALL BOY/布面丙烯/100cm×80cm/2008年

由郁至变态/DEPRESSION TO METAMORPHOSIS/布面丙烯/90cm×60cm/2008年

空中的梦想家／A DREAMER IN SKY／布面丙烯／100cm×80cm／2008年

两端/TWO SIDES/布面丙烯/100cm×80cm/2008年

笑忘书/FORGET LOVE WITH LAUGH/布面丙烯/130cm×180cm/2008年　（P89～P90）

幻想／FINAL FANTASY／布面丙烯／50cm×60cm／2008年　（P92～P93）

任天堂／HEAVEN／布面丙烯／90cm×60cm／2008年

衣靠／RELY ON／布面丙烯／100cm×80cm／2008年

太阳下的联想/CONNECT IN SUN'S MIND/布面丙烯/180cm×130cm/2008年

桔色之梦／DREAM WITH ORANGE／布面丙烯／50cm×60cm／2008年

中国女孩／CHINA GIRL／布面丙烯／90cm×60cm／2008年

功夫女孩／WORKMANSHIP GIRL／布面丙烯／100cm×80cm／2008年

天使也一样／ANGEL IS THE SAME／布面丙烯／60cm×50cm／2008年

简单爱/SIMPLE LOVE/布面丙烯/60cm×90cm/2008年

坐在气球上的女孩/A MISS ON THE BALLOON/布面丙烯/100cm×80cm/2008年

转机/TURN FOR BETTER/布面丙烯/90cm×60cm/2008年

闲云野鹤／FREE BOY／布面丙烯／130cm×180cm／2008年　（P109～P110）

花女孩/PURE MAIDEN GIRL/布面油画/80cm×100cm/2008年　(P112～P113)

你的责任／YOUR DUTY／布面丙烯／90cm×60cm／2008年

气男孩／HANDSOME　BOY／布面丙烯／90cm×60cm／2008年

因为有我/BECAUSE YOU HAVE ME/布面丙烯/100cm×100cm/2008年

国美人／CHINA BEAUTY／布面丙烯／100cm×100cm／2008年

三九天，我们也要在一起／THE BEST COLD DAYS, WE ARE IN TOGETHER AS BEFORE／布面丙烯／100cm×100cm／2008年

说傻话／SAY FOLLY／布面丙烯／100cm×100cm／2008年

复杂男孩／COMPLICATED BOY／布面丙烯／150cm×120cm／2008年

气泡的秘密／THE SECRET OF BUBBLE／布面丙烯／150cm×120cm／2008年

越长大越孤单／MORE AND MORE LONELY WITH GROW UP
布面丙烯／100cm×100cm／2008年

何处是我朋友的家/WHERE IS MY FRIENDS' HOUSEHOLD/布面丙烯/90cm×60cm/2008年

那些女孩教我的事/THE AFFAIRS INSTRUCT FOR ME FROM THOSE GIRLS/布面丙烯/100cm×80cm/2008年

绿发男孩／GREEN HAIR BOY／布面丙烯／60cm×90cm／2008年

青青白白／NATURE'S COLOR GIRL／布面丙烯／60cm×50cm／2008年

肉回家的青年/A YOUNG GOING HOME BOUGHT MEAT/布面丙烯/90cm×60cm/2008年

下学／FINISH CLASSES／布面丙烯／60cm×50cm／2008年

国美人／CHINA BEAUTY／布面丙烯／50cm×40cm／2008年

粉红假期/PINK HOLIDAY/布面丙烯/100cm×100cm/2008年

和你/WANT TO AND YOU IN TOGETHER/布面丙烯/150cm×120cm/2008年

遗失的美好/GLORIOUS STORYS FOR LOSE/布面丙烯/100cm×100cm/2008年

悔／HAVE NO REGRET／布面丙烯／100cm×100cm／2008年

雪人/YETI/布面丙烯/100cm×100cm/2008年

蓝紫之间／COLOR IN BLUE AND PURPLE／布面丙烯／100cm×80cm／2008年

一件小事／MINOR／布面丙烯／100cm×100cm／2008年

亚洲浪人／ASIA VAGRANT／布面丙烯／40cm×50cm／2008年

球男孩／TABLE TENNIS BOY／布面丙烯／60cm×90cm／2008年

反风向/TURN OVER THE DIRECTION OF WIND
布面丙烯/100cm×100cm/2008年

等爱的女孩／A GIRL IN WAITING LOVE／布面丙烯／100cm×100cm／2008年

短发/SHORT HAIR/布面丙烯/100cm×100cm/2008年

赤脚男孩／NAKED FOOT BOY／布面丙烯／60cm×50cm／2008年

海/THE OPEN SEA/布面丙烯/100cm×80cm/2008年

叛逆时期男孩／REBEL BOY／布面丙烯／90cm×60cm／2008年

发男孩／GREEN HAIR BOY／布面丙烯／50cm×60cm／2008年

54321／布面丙烯／60cm×50cm／2008年

斗星之梦/DREAM FOR THE PLOW/布面丙烯/60cm×50cm/2008年

小妇人的生活／LIFE FROM THE YOUNG MARRIED MISS／布面丙烯／90cm×60cm／2008年

初的人／THE FIRST LOVER IN LOVE／布面丙烯／150cm×120cm／2008年
∩TECOMERS／布面丙烯／40cm×50cm／2008年　（P154～P155）

爱比蔗糖甜/LOVE BETTER THAN SUCROSE/布面丙烯/50cm×40cm/2008年

想再听／NOT INTEND TO LISTEN／布面丙烯／150cm×120cm／2008年

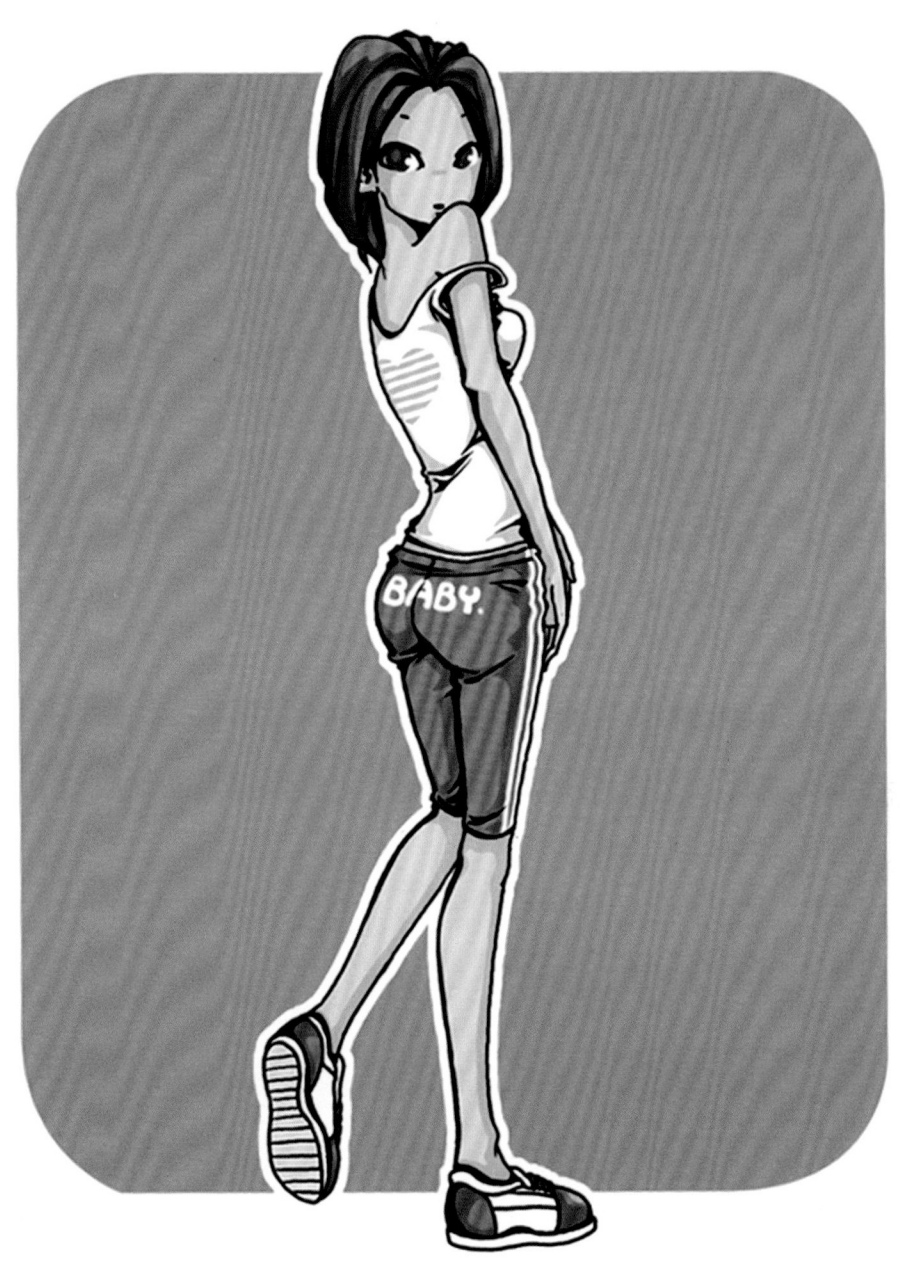

粉色心情／PINK MOOD／布面丙烯／100cm×80cm／2008年

兔女郎／MISS RABBIT／布面丙烯／100cm×80cm／2008年

图书在版编目(CIP)数据

中国当代艺术家画传/李梦绘.-石家庄：河北教育出版社，2008.10

ISBN 978-7-5434-6317-2

I.中... II.李... III.艺术家-评传-中国-现代-画册 IV.K825.7-64

中国版本图书馆CIP数据核字（2008）第069249号

出版发行 / 河北教育出版社
（石家庄市联盟路705号，邮编 050061）

出　　品 / 北京颂雅风文化艺术中心
北京市朝阳区北苑路172号3号楼2层，邮编 100101
电话 010-84853332

编辑总监 / 刘　峥

文字总监 / 郑一奇

责任编辑 / 张天漫

编辑助理 / 伍立君

设　　计 / 刘博扬

印　　制 / 北京方嘉彩色印刷有限责任公司

开　　本 / 787×1092　1/16　12印张

出版日期 / 2008年10月第1版　第1次印刷

书　　号 / ISBN 978-7-5434-6317-2

定　　价 / 58元